WITHDRAWN FROM
BEMIDJI PUBLIC LIBRARY

THE MALLARD

BY JEROLYN ANN NENTL

EDITED BY
DR. HOWARD SCHROEDER
Professor in Reading and Language Arts
Dept. of Elementary Education
Mankato State University

PRODUCED AND DESIGNED BY
BAKER STREET PRODUCTIONS
Mankato, MN

CRESTWOOD HOUSE
Mankato, Minnesota

LIBRARY OF CONGRESS CATALOGING IN PUBLICATION DATA
Nentl, Jerolyn Ann
  The mallard

  (Wildlife, habits and habitat)
  SUMMARY: Describes the physical characteristics, habits, and natural environment of the wild mallard duck, the ancestor of all the domestic ducks except the muscovy.
  1. Mallard--Juvenile literature. (1. Mallard. 2. Ducks) I. Schroeder, Howard. II. Title. III. Series.
QL696.A52N46   598.4'1   83-2087
ISBN 0-89686-221-6 (lib. bdg.)

International Standard Book Number:	Library of Congress Catalog Card Number:
Library Binding 0-89686-221-6	83-2087

ILLUSTRATION CREDITS:

Henry Kartarik: Cover
Lynn Rogers: 5, 8, 18, 21, 26, 29, 33, 36
Mark Ahlstrom: 6, 11, 13, 14, 31, 38, 40-41, 42
Bob Williams: 16, 17, 20, 30
Fish and Wildlife Service: 22
Sean Morgan: 24
Steve Kuchera: 34

Copyright© 1983 by Crestwood House, Inc. All rights reserved. No part of this book may be reproduced in any form without written permission from the publisher, except for brief passages included in a review. Printed in the United States of America.

Hwy. 66 South, Box 3427
Mankato, MN 56002-3427

TABLE OF CONTENTS

Introduction: 4

Chapter One: Where to find mallards 7
   Cold weather birds
   Shallow, still waters
   Prairie potholes
   Wildlife refuges

Chapter Two: What the mallards look like 12
   How the "greenhead" got its name
   A stocky bird

Chapter Three: How the mallards live 19
   Feeding
   Preening
   Molting

Chapter Four: The mallard's life cycle 25
   Early spring — choosing a mate
   The spring migration
   Late spring — making a nest
   Guarding the eggs
   Early summer — learning to live
   Late summer — getting together
   Fall — heading south
   Winter — waiting for spring

Chapter Five: The mallard's future 42
   Preserving wetlands
   Hunting

Map: Mallard country 45

Glossary: 46

INTRODUCTION:

In the morning quiet, a flock of birds flies around the tiny pond several times. They are high above the water. Necks are outstretched and green heads are held high, listening. When they are sure that the place is safe, they land with a rustle of wings. Once on the water they burst into action, shaking their feathers and beating their wings. They dip their bills and flip arcs of water over their backs, quacking loudly all the while. Then they waddle ashore and preen their feathers. Finally the birds settle down, tuck their heads under their wings and go to sleep.

These birds are mallards, one of the best-known ducks in the world. But only the male mallards, called drakes, have the green heads. The females, called ducks or hens, are a dull brown. (The proper term for the female is "duck;" but because that is confusing, we will use the common term, hen, in this book.)

Natural scientists call the mallard *Anas platyrhynchos*. It is a member of the large family of swimming birds called waterfowl. This family includes all ducks, geese, and swans. There are more than forty kinds, or species, of ducks. To help identify them, scientists place them in two groups according to how they find their food. Mallards are in the group called "dabblers" because they feed while staying on top of the water. Ducks in the second group are called "divers" because they dive beneath the surface of the water to get their food.

Ducks do not live as long as swans or geese. Most mallards live only eighteen months to five years.

The true mallards are wild ducks. By nature they are afraid of people and prefer a home where they can be left alone.

A small flock of mallards comes into a country pond.

A flock of mallards enjoys the pond in a city park.

There are millions of wild mallards in North America today. Since 1955, a late summer count has ranged from a low of thirteen million to a high of more than nineteen million. A count of mallards taken at that time of year is always at its highest. The ducklings have hatched and hunting has not yet started. Scientists can never be certain of the total number. It is very difficult to accurately count birds or animals living in the wild.

CHAPTER ONE:

Cold weather birds

Mallards are the most common of all ducks. Their range spans almost half the world, from the Tropic of Cancer in the south to the Arctic Circle in the North. There is hardly any place in the Northern Hemisphere where mallards are not seen at least some time during the year.

Mallards are migratory birds. This means they spend the winter in a different place than they spend the spring and summer. Long flights, northward in the spring and southward in the fall, take them from their wintering grounds to their breeding grounds, and back again, each year.

During their breeding times in the spring and summer, mallards are found in the northern and western United States. They are also found across most of Canada and throughout Alaska north to the Arctic Circle.

These North American mallards spend the winter most often in the southern United States, as far north as snow and ice allow. As long as they have food and open water, they don't mind cold temperatures. Sometimes they may migrate as far south as Mexico, Panama, and the West Indies, but this is rare.

Mallards also breed in northern Europe, Asia and Japan. These Eurasian mallards winter in southern Europe, Asia and northern Africa. They also have winter quarters in India, Burma, and Borneo.

Thus, the mallard is at home in almost the entire Northern Hemisphere. Mallards do not occur naturally in the Southern Hemisphere.

Mallards don't mind cold weather as long as they have food and open water.

Shallow, still waters

Mallards are freshwater birds. Usually they stay away from saltwater. Whether on their breeding or wintering grounds they prefer shallow, still water. They can be found on river deltas, marshes, sloughs, flooded meadows, and potholes. They can also be found around the edges of large lakes and rivers and on small streams and creeks. This habitat can be either natural or man-made. The mallards will live on either kind, as long as there is plenty of weeds and grass nearby. The plants give them food. They also hide them from predators.

Prairie potholes

One of the favorite breeding grounds of the mallards is the prairie pothole region. This area is in the north-central United States and south-central Canada. It covers about 300,000 square miles. Most of it is in the states of Montana, North Dakota, South Dakota and Minnesota, and in the provinces of Alberta, Saskatchewan and Manitoba.

This land is mostly flat with some gently rolling hills. Most geologists believe it was created thousands of years ago during the Ice Age by the glaciers that swept south from the far north. These moving masses of ice left behind thousands of low spots called potholes. Each year these potholes fill with water from the melting snow and heavy spring rains.

This prairie pothole region has the kind of habitat that mallards like best. There are so many mallards per square mile in this area that it is sometimes called "The Duck Factory."

Wildlife refuges

The largest flocks of mallards are often found in wildlife refuges and sanctuaries. These are large areas of protected land. Here birds and animals are left alone to live as they did years ago, before there were so many people. Some of these lands are owned by the government. Others are owned by organizations. A few are also owned by private citizens.

In the United States, government refuges are run by the Fish and Wildlife Service. The National Audubon Society is an example of a wildlife organization. It operates seventy-six sanctuaries. Local Audubon groups run one hundred more.

This prairie pothole in Saskatchewan is being used by both ducks and geese.

CHAPTER TWO:

How the "greenhead" got its name

No one who has seen the mallards can soon forget the drake's shiny green head. It glistens in the sunlight, making it an easy bird to identify. Yet the drake's head is not a true green at all. It is brown with a special colorless coating. This makes it look green to our eyes when the light hits it a certain way. True green pigment, or coloring matter, is rarely found in birds.

These shiny green feathers on the drake's head flow smoothly down his throat to a white band at his neck. His breast is a reddish brown, the color of chestnuts. His belly is white or gray. His back is darker gray blending to brown and ending in a glossy black rump. He has white tail feathers with two pairs of longer black feathers in the center. The black ones curl upward into a ringlet. His wings are dark gray to brown, with a patch of glowing blue or purple. This patch is called the speculum. It is bordered with narrow bands of first black and then white. He has orange feet and a dull yellow-green bill.

A mallard drake. Note the webbed feet.

A mallard hen, with a Canadian Honker in the background.

The hen is brown streaked with buff-yellow, gray, and black. This range of colors is often called mottled or spotted brown. She has glowing blue speculums and orange feet like the drake, but her bill is yellow-orange spotted with black. Her tail feathers are not curled and she has a distinct black eye stripe.

The familiar loud cries of "quack, quack-quack, quack" belong to the hen. The drake's call is a weaker, softer "kwek, kwek, kwek."

A stocky bird

A mallard is about two feet (62 cm) long from bill to tail and weighs about two and a half pounds (1.13 kg). Some may be as heavy as four pounds (1.81 kg). As a rule, the drake is slightly bigger than the hen. Mallards have long necks, wide bodies, short tails and short legs. They waddle when they walk, pointing each foot inward toward the middle.

Like all ducks, a mallard's three front toes are webbed. A fourth, smaller toe is in the back and slightly above the others. This fourth toe has no webbing and appears to serve no useful purpose. It is the webbing between the three front toes that helps make ducks such good swimmers. But webbing can hinder their walking when on land.

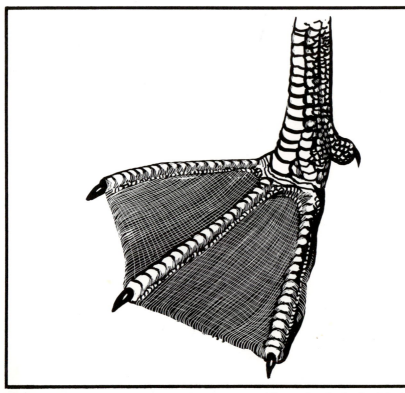

Webbed feet make ducks good swimmers. They also help the birds to land and take-off from water.

    A mallard's bill is wide and flat, and it has a round tip. The two parts of the bill are called the mandibles. The edges of each mandible are serrated like the cutting edge of a saw. The outside of the bill has a soft covering except for the tip of the upper mandible. This tip is a hooked hard spot. A mallard's tongue is thick. It also has serrated edges. The ser-

This drawing shows the serrated edges on a mallard's bill and tongue.

rated edges on the bill and tongue help the mallard to get and eat food.

A mallard's wings are very powerful. These ducks are strong, fast flyers and can fly for a long time. They can launch themselves directly into the air from either land or water. One giant downward stroke of their outstretched wings, plus a push with their feet, gets them going.

To land, mallards rear back almost upright. They hold their heads high and spread their tails, wings and webbed feet to break their speed and guide their descent. Beating their wings forward also helps break their speed. This is sometimes called backflapping. They stretch their legs forward and bend them as they hit the water or the ground for an easy landing.

Mallards are almost in an upright position when they take-off and land.

CHAPTER THREE:

Most of a mallard's time is spent eating, sleeping and preening its plumage, or feathers.

Mallards are gregarious birds. This means that they are very sociable. Whatever they do is done in pairs, small groups, or flocks, except during nesting time. They often feed and preen with other birds, especially other kinds of ducks.

Feeding

Mallards feed widely on aquatic plants and animals. They prefer the leaves, berries and tender new shoots of waterplants. But they will also eat the stems, seeds and even the roots. Wetland areas provide them with plenty of grasses and other waterplants. Mallards like smartweeds, pondweeds, duckweeds, coontail, wild celery, water elm and wapato. Ninety per cent of their diet consists of this kind of plant food, plus grain in the fall and winter. The other ten per cent is made up of animal matter such as insects, tadpoles, small fish, fish eggs, worms and snails. Nesting hens and ducklings eat just the

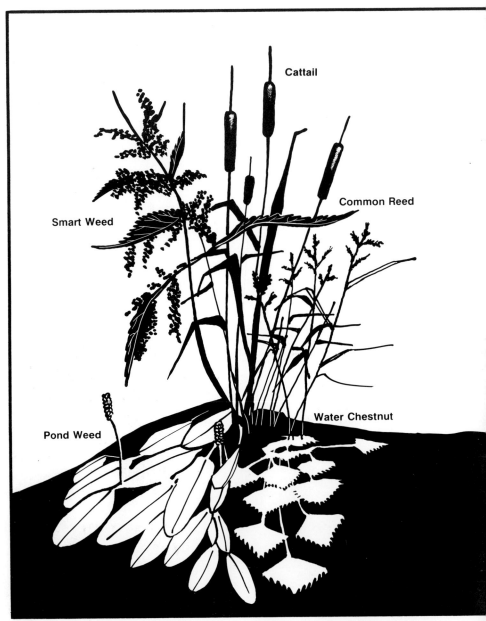

These water plants are some of the mallard's favorite foods.

opposite. They eat mostly insects and other animal matter.

Mallards feed while on top of the water. They do this by tipping up on end and paddling as fast as they can. Paddling helps keep their rumps in the air while they swish their bills through the water. This "bottoms up" type of feeding is called dabbling.

During the fall and winter months, mallards also flock to stubble fields to feed on leftover grain. They like corn the best, but they will feed on wheat, oats and barley, too. In the South, they can also be found in the rice and sorghum fields. Mallards may fly many miles morning and night to feed in these fields.

Bottoms up! This drake is "dabbling" for food under the water.

Sometimes they start feeding in the fields before harvest. Then this field feeding can become a problem for farmers. A large drake can eat up to four hundred kernels of corn in one sitting.

Preening

Preening may be one of the most important things mallards do. It keeps them clean, warm and dry.

Preening simply means smoothing the feathers. A mallard shakes its body from tail to head and then uses its bill to smooth the ruffled feathers. While doing this, the bill passes over a gland that produces oil. This gland is at the base of the tail. As the

While preening, this mallard can also get rid of bugs and other insects that might be on him.

mallard smooths its feathers with its bill it also spreads the oil. Rubbing its chin and neck on its body helps to spread the oil, too. This oil is what keeps the mallard's feathers waterproof. While preening, the mallard also removes insects with its bill.

Sometimes mallards are sick or hurt and cannot preen their feathers. If they don't, the oil wears off. Then water can seep through to their skin and they get cold. If their body temperature drops too low for a long time, they may die.

Molting

Molting is the yearly loss and regrowth of a bird's feathers. It is done to replace feathers that might be damaged. For mallards, molting occurs twice each year. It happens once during the early summer months and again late in the summer. The molting process takes about a month each time. Scientists call this a double annual molt.

The drake first molts his colorful body feathers, called his "nuptial plumage." This happens in early summer. The new growth of feathers is called his "eclipse plumage." These feathers are spotted brown. With them, he looks much like the hen. About the only way to tell them apart during this time is by the curl of his tail and the black spots on her bill.

The drake's eclipse plumage lasts for a month or more during mid-summer. During this time the drake sheds his wing, or flight, feathers. Without them, he cannot fly. For safety, the drakes gather on open water, and feed during mid-day rather than at dawn or dusk. The only way for them to escape danger is to dive beneath the water or to swim away and hide. The dull colors of their eclipse plumage help to hide them during this flightless time.

In late summer the drake molts his body feathers again. This time he loses the dull brown feathers of the eclipse plumage. He regains his colorful nuptial plumage.

The hen also has a double annual molt of her feathers. It is not as noticeable as the drake's because her basic color does not change as much. As a rule, she molts at her nesting area. For awhile she is also flightless, like the drake.

Mallards spend much time hiding while they are flightless. This drake has started to get back his nuptial plumage, and will soon be able to fly.

CHAPTER FOUR:

Each year mallards mate, build their nests, raise their ducklings and molt their feathers. These events are timed around the mallard's two migration flights. Mallards most often choose their mates on their wintering grounds in the south. They build their nests, raise their ducklings and molt on their breeding grounds in the north.

Early spring — choosing a mate

Mallards choose their mates in late winter and early spring before they leave their wintering grounds.

The drakes display their plumage with a great show! They shake their heads and tails and curve their necks. They puff up their feathers and dip their bills into the water, throwing it over their shoulders. All the while, they make strange noises that sound like whistles and grunts. Each drake wants to attract a hen to be his mate.

The hens urge on the drakes, giving them quite a

A drake chases after a hen during their courtship.

chase. They shake their heads and dip their bills in the water, swimming around first one drake and then another. Then the drakes turn around and chase the hens. If chased too closely before she is ready to choose a mate, a hen may take flight. The drakes will follow her, soaring high overhead and then sweeping very low toward the water. Back and forth they go, soaring and diving.

Courtship can go on like this for several weeks, most often on crisp sunny mornings. When a hen has finally made her choice, she lets the drake know by swimming up to him. They face each other, dip their bills in the water and drink. To an observer, it can almost look as if they are bowing to each other. Then, they swim off together as a pair for that breeding season. Next year there will be another courtship display by the drakes. The hens will again choose their mates, but they might not be the same mate as before.

The spring migration

Mallard pairs, or mates, make the spring migration flight northward to their breeding grounds together. The hen leads, with the drake following after her. As a rule, a mallard hen returns each year to the area where she was hatched.

Mallards fly in small flocks on these northward flights. These flights occur from February to May. As a rule, all mallards have arrived at their breeding grounds each year by the middle of May.

Once at their breeding grounds, the pairs go off two by two. They feed and swim together. They stay away from other birds, losing for awhile their usual social nature. It is during this time that actual breeding occurs.

As a rule, each pair stays within a home range. This area will have plenty of food and water, plus nesting cover for the hen. It will also have an area a short distance from the nesting site for the drake to use. The drake protects his mate, giving chase if she is attacked by another duck. He does not defend the borders of their home range as do some birds and animals.

Late spring — making a nest

Locating a place for the nest is the hen's job. She looks the land over early each morning with much loud quacking. The drake goes with her on this daily search. Most often she settles for a site on the ground near the water's edge. It is best if the spot is sheltered by tall grasses, reeds or other plants.

A mallard's bill is not made for carrying things. To build a nest, the hen simply sits down. Then she reaches out to pluck whatever plants are close around her. With a flip of her bill she tosses them over her shoulder. She does this while turning around in a circle and kicking her feet. This forms a nest bowl. As she continues, she also plucks some of the down from her breast. This falls into the bowl and becomes part of the nest, too. Making a nest from the natural growth around it helps to keep it hidden from predators.

The hen likes tall grasses in which to build her nest.

A mallard hen usually lays a group, or clutch, of eight to ten eggs. At times there may be as many as fifteen or as few as five. Mallard eggs have smooth shells and range in color from pale green to white. They are oblong in shape, with one end larger than the other. The hen lays one egg a day, making a trip to the nest early each morning. The drake goes along on these daily trips to the nest, too. Each day, the hen

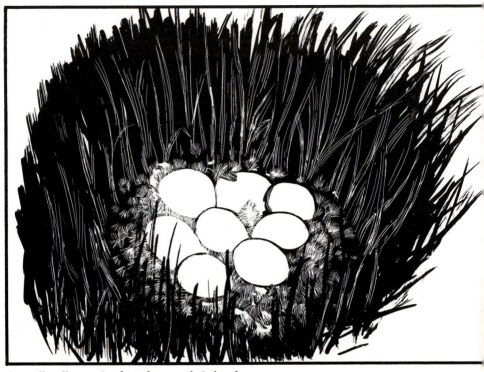
A mallard's nest, showing a clutch of eggs.

plucks a little more down from her breast to help hide the newest egg. This also helps keep them warm. The eggs need to be kept warm to develop properly.

To get them to hatch, the hen sits on them, using her body to warm the eggs. This is called incubation. In the wild, incubation takes about twenty-eight days. The hen does not begin to incubate her clutch until the last egg is laid. A week or more may pass from the time the first egg is laid until she starts to incubate them. This waiting allows all the eggs in the clutch to hatch at about the same time.

Most of the time the drake just loafs, waiting for his mate to leave the nest and join him to feed and preen. He soon tires of this. He protects her less and less, and he begins to wander farther to feed. He often chases other females. This may be how he got the name "mallard," which means "the very male one" or "the wild one." If he breeds with hens of other species, the ducklings produced are called hybrids. Hybrids often occur in the wild, but they are never able to reproduce.

Two drakes are in the center of the photo. The one on the right is a hybrid.

At last he and all the other drakes from that nesting area fly off to find a new feeding ground for themselves. Their job completed, they begin to molt.

Guarding the eggs

There are many predators who would like to make a quick meal of a duck egg. Some of them are other birds, such as crows or gulls. Others are animals, such as raccoons, coyotes, foxes or ground squirrels.

A hen can be very brave in defense of her eggs if she has been incubating them awhile. She will defend them with much quacking and wing-flapping. She will turn on her own mate, if she thinks he is a threat. Often a hen will fake illness or injury to lure the enemy away from her nest. Yet if there is a threat to a freshly-laid clutch of eggs, the hen may simply abandon both the eggs and the nest. She is not yet attached enough to a fresh clutch to care much about the eggs. If a hen loses her clutch of eggs to a predator or to the weather, she may mate again.

Not all of the eggs laid by a hen in a breeding season will hatch. In addition to those destroyed by predators, some eggs are not fertile. A few eggs may be destroyed by disease or bad weather. A late frost or flood can also destroy many duck eggs. So can a hailstorm.

A mallard duckling explores its new world.

Ducklings begin to cheep from within the shell of the surviving eggs before they hatch. It is quite a struggle for the ducklings to peck their way out of the eggs. It may take them a few days.

When they hatch, their eyes are open and they are covered with a soft coat of fuzz called natal down. Birds that are hatched well-developed, like ducklings, are called precocial.

A duckling's underparts and the sides of its head are yellow. Its upperparts are brown and it has brown eye and cheek stripes. There are two yellow spots on its shoulders and two on its rump. These colors are quite bright when a duckling first hatches but fade as it grows older. The male and female ducklings look very much alike. It is difficult to tell them apart until they get their adult feathers.

The ducklings are very sensitive for the first day or so after hatching. The hen knows this by instinct and stays on her nest during this time. This is the way she makes sure they learn that she is their mother. Then they will have no trouble recognizing her or following her. This is called imprinting. It is not good to take a duckling from its mother or the nest during this time.

Ducklings are able to walk and to swim almost from the time they hatch. They can forage, or look for food, by themselves within a few hours of hatching. However, the hen keeps them in the nest for the first night. This is part of the imprinting time. Then she leads them to the nearest water the next day.

The brood goes for a swim.

Early summer — learning to live

The little family does not return to the nest. The brood needs space to learn about the world. The ducklings will keep in touch with one another by their constant peeping. If they sense danger, their peeps will become loud and shrill.

For the first few nights the hen gathers her brood around her to warm them. During the day she teaches them to catch insects and to hide from predators, or animals who would eat them. The ducklings soon have no need to sleep next to the hen for warmth. They seem to know by instinct what to do. Yet the hen stays with them most of the summer to guide them.

Ducklings can fall victim to many of the same predators that preyed on the eggs. Once the ducklings are on the water, snapping turtles and bullfrogs may also prey on them. Big fish like pike and carp may feed on small ducklings at times, too. Even cats and dogs will kill them.

At the first sign of danger the hen gives a screech of alarm. The ducklings scatter in all directions. They may hide in the brush or dive beneath the surface of the water. Meanwhile, she tries to attract the attention of the predator in the same ways that she kept enemies away from her eggs.

By the time a duckling is about three weeks old, it

These ducklings, living in the city with their mother, have their juvenal plumage.

begins to get its feathers. This first set of body feathers is called a duckling's juvenal plumage. They are smaller, softer feathers than those of the adults. These body feathers are spotted brown, and the ducklings all look very much like their mother.

Their wing or flight feathers are not complete until the end of the summer when they are about ten weeks old. Once these feathers are in, they are able to fly. At this time, the young ducks, called "fledglings," go their separate ways. They can look out for themselves and no longer need their mother.

A duckling's juvenal plumage does not last for long. The ducklings molt these body feathers in late summer. This is when the male ducklings finally begin to get their distinctive colors. By the next spring the ducklings will have become adult birds. They will get their own mates and be able to rear a brood of ducklings of their own.

Late summer — getting together

Thousands of mallard drakes and hens flock together during the late summer months each year to feed and rest. They are getting themselves ready for the fall migration flight southward. This mass gathering is called staging. Joining the older ducks are the ducklings that hatched in the spring. They are now called birds-of-the-year.

The mallards gather wherever there is an abundance of food. Sometimes they will move several hundred miles away from their home range. These places where they gather are called staging areas. The mallards begin, or stage, their fall migration from these mass feeding areas.

Fall — heading south

The great flocks of migrating birds is a beautiful sight to see. One hears them first — the quacking of the ducks and the honking of the geese. The sounds are faint, then louder and louder as they pass overhead. They may be in long lines or in U and V formations. At times they fly almost wing-to-wing.

Scientists do not know for sure how the migration instinct works. They do know that changes in the weather help birds, such as mallards, know when it is time to migrate. When the air turns crisp and the water begins to freeze, the mallards know it is time to move southward. Food is getting scarce. The

A flock of mallards heads south.

amount of daylight and the movements of the sun also seem to tell them when to migrate and how to find their way. So do star patterns at night.

Yet there are a few mallards that live the year-around in milder climates such as the Pacific Northwest. The temperature is right all year in these places for mallards to thrive. It never gets so cold that there is no food. Here they breed and winter in the same general area.

The mallards breeding in colder climates migrate southward from September through November. These mallards like to stay as far north as they can for as long as they can. They linger at choice feeding areas.

Some may fly as far as three thousand miles. Because the young ducks aren't strong yet, they stop often to feed and rest. There are often thousands of ducks in these migrating flocks.

Whether flying northward or southward, mallards follow the age-old routes used by all migrating birds. These routes are called flyways. Four of them are in North America. Two are along the coastlines and two reach across the center of the continent. The Atlantic Flyway follows the east coast of Canada and the United States. The Pacific Flyway follows the west coast and the Rocky Mountains. The Mississippi Flyway follows that long river to the Gulf of Mexico. So many mallards use the Mississippi route that it is sometimes called "The Mallard Flyway."

Thousands of mallards ready to land in a stubble field.

The Central Flyway is along a line from northeast Alaska southward across the Northwest Territories to the Texas Coast. Some birds using this route continue into Mexico.

Winter — waiting for spring

Mallards reach their winter quarters by the end of November. They gather wherever it is warm enough

not to freeze their water habitat. Snow and ice must not cover their food supply or they will starve before spring. Surprisingly, some mallards winter in Alaska! Hot springs in parts of the interior of that state keep some waters ice-free all year.

It is on these wintering grounds that the mallards wait for the ice and snow on their breeding grounds in the north to melt. By late winter the drakes start their courtship of the hens. Then the yearly cycle of breeding and migrating begins again.

CHAPTER FIVE:

Preserving wetlands

A nesting hen may be in danger from predators or the weather at any time, as may mallards weak from

It's wetlands like these that need to be preserved if we're to have large numbers of mallards in the future.

hunger or sickness. The rest of the adult mallards have few natural enemies.

The mallard's main enemy is mankind. People are destroying the wetlands where the mallards breed.

Presently the mallard is in no danger of extinction. But the number of wild mallards has decreased in this century. Many of the mallard's best wetland breeding grounds are being drained or filled. When this happens the mallards have no place to feed or breed.

If mallards are to thrive in future years, the remaining wetlands must be preserved. Those lost should be reclaimed or new ones must be created. Land preservation takes much money, time and effort. One good example of what can be done is the effort being made by Ducks Unlimited, Inc. During the past fifty years this group has preserved or created nearly three million acres of wetlands in North America.

People can help determine how many mallards will survive in the future. They can prevent pollution of the land and water. They can make sure that farms and cities do not use up all the prime wetland breeding areas.

Hunting

People do not need to kill birds and animals for food today. Hunting is now done mainly for sport. The mallard is one of the hunter's prized game birds.

Hunters have to buy a license in each state or province in order to hunt there. Many states also require hunters to buy a state duck stamp. Each hunter in the United States must also purchase a Federal Duck Stamp each season. Most of the money from the sale of licenses and duck stamps goes toward the preservation of wetland breeding grounds.

Hunting is controlled today mainly by the use of seasons and bag limits. Certain days and times are set aside each year when hunting is allowed. This time is called the waterfowl hunting season. Only certain kinds of ducks and a certain number of them may be shot during this time. Such hunting controls help make sure that too many birds will never be killed in one season. These controls, along with preservation and wise use of the wetland breeding grounds, can help ensure the survival of the mallards. Then future generations will also be able to enjoy the hunt or watch a flock of mallards alight on a pond to feed on a crisp spring morning.

MAP:

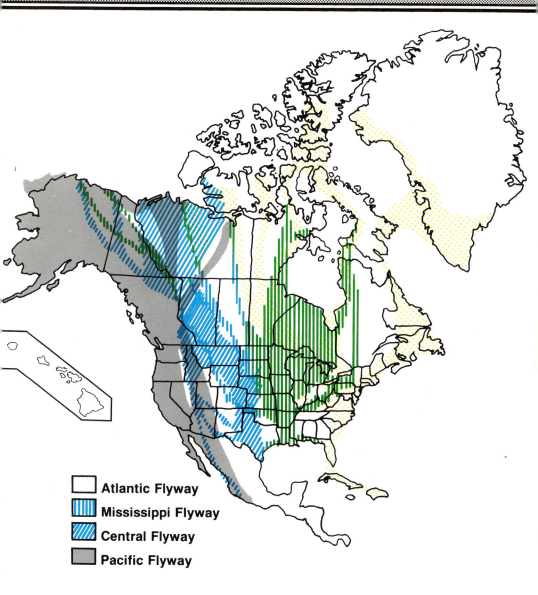

- Atlantic Flyway
- Mississippi Flyway
- Central Flyway
- Pacific Flyway

GLOSSARY:

BROOD - A group of birds hatched at one time and cared for together.

CLUTCH - A nest of eggs.

DABBLING - To dip lightly in and out of the water.

DOWN - Soft, fine feathers.

ECLIPSE PLUMAGE - The set of feathers some birds have between breeding seasons.

FLEDGLINGS - A young duck that is able to fly for the first time.

GAME BIRD - Wild birds hunted for sport or for use as food.

HABITAT - The place where a plant or animal lives.

HYBRID - The offspring of two birds of different species.

IMPRINT - To impress firmly upon the mind; to fix firmly in the memory.

INCUBATE - To sit upon the eggs, keeping them warm, so they will develop properly and hatch.

INSTINCT - A tendency that a bird has when it is hatched to behave in a way special to that species.

MANDIBLE - Either part of a bird's beak or bill.

MIGRATE - To move from one region to another with the change of seasons.

MOLT - To cast off or shed the feathers at certain times and replace them with new growth.

NUPTIAL PLUMAGE - The set of feathers a bird has during the breeding season.

PIGMENT - The coloring matter in the cells and tissues of plants and animals.

PLUMAGE - A bird's feathers.

PREDATOR - An animal that hunts and kills other animals (called prey) for food.

PREEN - To clean and smooth the feathers with the beak or bill.

PREY - An animal hunted and killed by another animal for food.

REFUGE - A place of safety.

SANCTUARY - A place where animals and birds are sheltered from harm so they can breed.

SERRATED - Having notches along the edge like a saw.

SPECULUM - A distinct patch of color on the wings of certain birds, especially ducks.

STAGING AREA - The place where birds gather before beginning their fall migration flight.

WILDLIFE
HABITS & HABITAT

READ AND ENJOY THE SERIES:

THE WHITETAIL
THE BALD EAGLE
THE WOLVES
THE PHEASANT
THE BEAVER
THE MALLARD
THE FOXES
THE SQUIRRELS